50 Savory Pancake Recipes

By: Kelly Johnson

Table of Contents

- Classic Potato Pancakes
- Zucchini Fritters
- Cornmeal Pancakes with Jalapeños
- Spinach and Feta Pancakes
- Savory Oatmeal Pancakes
- Carrot and Onion Pancakes
- Chickpea Flour Pancakes (Besan Chilla)
- Savory Ricotta Pancakes
- Sweet Potato Pancakes with Chives
- Cauliflower Pancakes
- Mushroom and Thyme Pancakes
- Broccoli and Cheddar Pancakes
- Kimchi Pancakes (Kimchi Jeon)
- Beetroot Pancakes
- Savory Dutch Baby Pancake
- Herb and Cheese Pancakes
- Bacon and Corn Pancakes
- Thai-Style Shrimp Pancakes
- Salmon and Dill Pancakes
- Savory Pumpkin Pancakes
- Leek and Potato Pancakes
- Cabbage Pancakes
- Quinoa Pancakes with Spinach
- Eggplant and Mozzarella Pancakes
- Methi Thepla (Fenugreek Flatbreads)
- Savory Yogurt Pancakes
- Thai Scallion Pancakes
- Italian Polenta Pancakes
- Prawn and Chive Pancakes
- Savory Tomato Pancakes
- Couscous and Vegetable Pancakes
- Black Bean Pancakes
- Savory Crêpes with Ham and Cheese
- Tandoori Chicken Pancakes
- Spinach and Ricotta Pancakes

- Savory Pancakes with Roasted Red Peppers
- Pesto and Parmesan Pancakes
- Savory Pancakes with Olive Tapenade
- Radish Pancakes
- Celeriac and Herb Pancakes
- Sweet Corn and Zucchini Pancakes
- Savory Pancakes with Greek Yogurt Sauce
- Fennel and Orange Pancakes
- Chard and Cheese Pancakes
- Coconut Curry Pancakes
- Bacon and Chive Pancakes
- Savory Pancakes with Avocado and Salsa
- Mushroom and Spinach Pancakes
- Savory Pancakes with Tomato Chutney
- Green Onion and Bacon Pancakes

Classic Potato Pancakes

Ingredients:

- 4 medium potatoes (peeled and grated)
- 1 small onion (finely chopped)
- 2 eggs
- 1/4 cup all-purpose flour
- Salt and pepper to taste
- Oil for frying

Instructions:

1. Squeeze excess moisture from grated potatoes and onion.
2. In a bowl, combine potatoes, onion, eggs, flour, salt, and pepper.
3. Heat oil in a skillet over medium heat.
4. Drop spoonfuls of the mixture into the skillet and flatten slightly.
5. Fry until golden brown on both sides. Drain on paper towels before serving.

Zucchini Fritters

Ingredients:

- 2 medium zucchinis (grated)
- 1/2 cup all-purpose flour
- 1/4 cup grated Parmesan cheese
- 1 egg
- Salt and pepper to taste
- Oil for frying

Instructions:

1. Squeeze excess moisture from grated zucchini.
2. In a bowl, combine zucchini, flour, cheese, egg, salt, and pepper.
3. Heat oil in a skillet over medium heat.
4. Drop spoonfuls of the mixture into the skillet and flatten slightly.
5. Fry until golden brown on both sides. Drain on paper towels before serving.

Cornmeal Pancakes with Jalapeños

Ingredients:

- 1 cup cornmeal
- 1 cup milk
- 1 egg
- 1/4 cup chopped jalapeños
- 1 teaspoon baking powder
- Salt to taste
- Oil for frying

Instructions:

1. In a bowl, mix cornmeal, milk, egg, jalapeños, baking powder, and salt.
2. Heat oil in a skillet over medium heat.
3. Pour batter onto the skillet and cook until bubbles form on the surface.
4. Flip and cook until golden brown. Drain on paper towels before serving.

Spinach and Feta Pancakes

Ingredients:

- 1 cup fresh spinach (chopped)
- 1/2 cup crumbled feta cheese
- 1 cup all-purpose flour
- 2 eggs
- 1 cup milk
- Salt and pepper to taste
- Oil for frying

Instructions:

1. In a bowl, combine spinach, feta, flour, eggs, milk, salt, and pepper.
2. Heat oil in a skillet over medium heat.
3. Pour batter onto the skillet and cook until bubbles form on the surface.
4. Flip and cook until golden brown. Drain on paper towels before serving.

Savory Oatmeal Pancakes

Ingredients:

- 1 cup rolled oats
- 1 cup buttermilk
- 1 egg
- 1/2 cup grated cheese (optional)
- Salt and pepper to taste
- Oil for frying

Instructions:

1. In a bowl, combine oats, buttermilk, egg, cheese, salt, and pepper.
2. Heat oil in a skillet over medium heat.
3. Pour batter onto the skillet and cook until bubbles form on the surface.
4. Flip and cook until golden brown. Drain on paper towels before serving.

Carrot and Onion Pancakes

Ingredients:

- 2 medium carrots (grated)
- 1 small onion (finely chopped)
- 2 eggs
- 1/2 cup all-purpose flour
- Salt and pepper to taste
- Oil for frying

Instructions:

1. In a bowl, combine carrots, onion, eggs, flour, salt, and pepper.
2. Heat oil in a skillet over medium heat.
3. Drop spoonfuls of the mixture into the skillet and flatten slightly.
4. Fry until golden brown on both sides. Drain on paper towels before serving.

Chickpea Flour Pancakes (Besan Chilla)

Ingredients:

- 1 cup chickpea flour (besan)
- 1 cup water
- 1/4 cup chopped onions
- 1/4 cup chopped tomatoes
- Salt and spices to taste
- Oil for frying

Instructions:

1. In a bowl, mix chickpea flour, water, onions, tomatoes, salt, and spices.
2. Heat oil in a skillet over medium heat.
3. Pour batter onto the skillet and spread evenly.
4. Cook until the edges lift, then flip and cook until golden. Drain on paper towels before serving.

Savory Ricotta Pancakes

Ingredients:

- 1 cup ricotta cheese
- 2 eggs
- 1/2 cup all-purpose flour
- Salt and pepper to taste
- Oil for frying

Instructions:

1. In a bowl, combine ricotta, eggs, flour, salt, and pepper.
2. Heat oil in a skillet over medium heat.
3. Drop spoonfuls of the mixture into the skillet and flatten slightly.
4. Fry until golden brown on both sides. Drain on paper towels before serving.

Sweet Potato Pancakes with Chives

Ingredients:

- 1 cup mashed sweet potatoes
- 2 eggs
- 1/2 cup all-purpose flour
- 1/4 cup chopped chives
- Salt and pepper to taste
- Oil for frying

Instructions:

1. In a bowl, combine sweet potatoes, eggs, flour, chives, salt, and pepper.
2. Heat oil in a skillet over medium heat.
3. Drop spoonfuls of the mixture into the skillet and flatten slightly.
4. Fry until golden brown on both sides. Drain on paper towels before serving.

Cauliflower Pancakes

Ingredients:

- 1 head of cauliflower (riced)
- 1/2 cup all-purpose flour
- 2 eggs
- Salt and pepper to taste
- Oil for frying

Instructions:

1. Steam the riced cauliflower until tender, then drain and cool.
2. In a bowl, combine cauliflower, flour, eggs, salt, and pepper.
3. Heat oil in a skillet over medium heat.
4. Drop spoonfuls of the mixture into the skillet and flatten slightly.
5. Fry until golden brown on both sides. Drain on paper towels before serving.

Mushroom and Thyme Pancakes

Ingredients:

- 1 cup mushrooms (finely chopped)
- 1/2 cup all-purpose flour
- 2 eggs
- 1 teaspoon fresh thyme (chopped)
- Salt and pepper to taste
- Oil for frying

Instructions:

1. Sauté mushrooms in a pan until softened.
2. In a bowl, combine mushrooms, flour, eggs, thyme, salt, and pepper.
3. Heat oil in a skillet over medium heat.
4. Drop spoonfuls of the mixture into the skillet and flatten slightly.
5. Fry until golden brown on both sides. Drain on paper towels before serving.

Broccoli and Cheddar Pancakes

Ingredients:

- 1 cup broccoli (chopped and steamed)
- 1/2 cup shredded cheddar cheese
- 1/2 cup all-purpose flour
- 2 eggs
- Salt and pepper to taste
- Oil for frying

Instructions:

1. In a bowl, combine broccoli, cheddar, flour, eggs, salt, and pepper.
2. Heat oil in a skillet over medium heat.
3. Drop spoonfuls of the mixture into the skillet and flatten slightly.
4. Fry until golden brown on both sides. Drain on paper towels before serving.

Kimchi Pancakes (Kimchi Jeon)

Ingredients:

- 1 cup kimchi (chopped)
- 1/2 cup all-purpose flour
- 1 egg
- 1/4 cup water
- Green onions (optional)
- Oil for frying

Instructions:

1. In a bowl, mix kimchi, flour, egg, water, and green onions.
2. Heat oil in a skillet over medium heat.
3. Pour batter onto the skillet and spread evenly.
4. Cook until golden brown on both sides. Drain on paper towels before serving.

Beetroot Pancakes

Ingredients:

- 1 cup cooked beetroot (pureed)
- 1/2 cup all-purpose flour
- 2 eggs
- Salt and pepper to taste
- Oil for frying

Instructions:

1. In a bowl, combine beetroot, flour, eggs, salt, and pepper.
2. Heat oil in a skillet over medium heat.
3. Drop spoonfuls of the mixture into the skillet and flatten slightly.
4. Fry until golden brown on both sides. Drain on paper towels before serving.

Savory Dutch Baby Pancake

Ingredients:

- 3 eggs
- 1 cup milk
- 1 cup all-purpose flour
- 1 teaspoon salt
- 1 tablespoon butter
- Herbs and cheese (optional)

Instructions:

1. Preheat oven to 425°F (220°C).
2. In a bowl, whisk together eggs, milk, flour, and salt.
3. Melt butter in a cast-iron skillet in the oven.
4. Pour batter into the hot skillet and bake for 20-25 minutes until puffed.
5. Serve with herbs and cheese if desired.

Herb and Cheese Pancakes

Ingredients:

- 1 cup all-purpose flour
- 1 cup milk
- 1 cup shredded cheese (your choice)
- 2 eggs
- Fresh herbs (chopped)
- Salt and pepper to taste
- Oil for frying

Instructions:

1. In a bowl, mix flour, milk, cheese, eggs, herbs, salt, and pepper.
2. Heat oil in a skillet over medium heat.
3. Drop spoonfuls of the mixture into the skillet and flatten slightly.
4. Fry until golden brown on both sides. Drain on paper towels before serving.

Bacon and Corn Pancakes

Ingredients:

- 1 cup corn kernels (fresh or canned)
- 1/2 cup cooked bacon (crumbled)
- 1 cup all-purpose flour
- 2 eggs
- 1/2 cup milk
- Salt and pepper to taste
- Oil for frying

Instructions:

1. In a bowl, combine corn, bacon, flour, eggs, milk, salt, and pepper.
2. Heat oil in a skillet over medium heat.
3. Drop spoonfuls of the mixture into the skillet and flatten slightly.
4. Fry until golden brown on both sides. Drain on paper towels before serving.

Thai-Style Shrimp Pancakes

Ingredients:

- 1 cup shrimp (chopped)
- 1/2 cup all-purpose flour
- 2 eggs
- 1 tablespoon fish sauce
- 1 tablespoon cilantro (chopped)
- Oil for frying

Instructions:

1. In a bowl, combine shrimp, flour, eggs, fish sauce, and cilantro.
2. Heat oil in a skillet over medium heat.
3. Drop spoonfuls of the mixture into the skillet and flatten slightly.
4. Fry until golden brown on both sides. Drain on paper towels before serving.

Salmon and Dill Pancakes

Ingredients:

- 1 cup cooked salmon (flaked)
- 1/2 cup all-purpose flour
- 2 eggs
- 1 tablespoon fresh dill (chopped)
- Salt and pepper to taste
- Oil for frying

Instructions:

1. In a bowl, combine salmon, flour, eggs, dill, salt, and pepper.
2. Heat oil in a skillet over medium heat.
3. Drop spoonfuls of the mixture into the skillet and flatten slightly.
4. Fry until golden brown on both sides. Drain on paper towels before serving.

Savory Pumpkin Pancakes

Ingredients:

- 1 cup pumpkin puree
- 1/2 cup all-purpose flour
- 2 eggs
- 1 teaspoon baking powder
- Salt and pepper to taste
- Oil for frying

Instructions:

1. In a bowl, mix pumpkin puree, flour, eggs, baking powder, salt, and pepper until smooth.
2. Heat oil in a skillet over medium heat.
3. Drop spoonfuls of the mixture into the skillet and flatten slightly.
4. Fry until golden brown on both sides. Drain on paper towels before serving.

Leek and Potato Pancakes

Ingredients:

- 1 cup potatoes (grated)
- 1 cup leeks (finely chopped)
- 1/2 cup all-purpose flour
- 2 eggs
- Salt and pepper to taste
- Oil for frying

Instructions:

1. In a bowl, combine grated potatoes, leeks, flour, eggs, salt, and pepper.
2. Heat oil in a skillet over medium heat.
3. Drop spoonfuls of the mixture into the skillet and flatten slightly.
4. Fry until golden brown on both sides. Drain on paper towels before serving.

Cabbage Pancakes

Ingredients:

- 2 cups cabbage (shredded)
- 1/2 cup all-purpose flour
- 2 eggs
- Salt and pepper to taste
- Oil for frying

Instructions:

1. In a bowl, combine shredded cabbage, flour, eggs, salt, and pepper.
2. Heat oil in a skillet over medium heat.
3. Drop spoonfuls of the mixture into the skillet and flatten slightly.
4. Fry until golden brown on both sides. Drain on paper towels before serving.

Quinoa Pancakes with Spinach

Ingredients:

- 1 cup cooked quinoa
- 1 cup spinach (chopped)
- 1/2 cup all-purpose flour
- 2 eggs
- Salt and pepper to taste
- Oil for frying

Instructions:

1. In a bowl, combine quinoa, spinach, flour, eggs, salt, and pepper.
2. Heat oil in a skillet over medium heat.
3. Drop spoonfuls of the mixture into the skillet and flatten slightly.
4. Fry until golden brown on both sides. Drain on paper towels before serving.

Eggplant and Mozzarella Pancakes

Ingredients:

- 1 cup eggplant (cooked and mashed)
- 1/2 cup mozzarella cheese (shredded)
- 1/2 cup all-purpose flour
- 2 eggs
- Salt and pepper to taste
- Oil for frying

Instructions:

1. In a bowl, combine mashed eggplant, mozzarella, flour, eggs, salt, and pepper.
2. Heat oil in a skillet over medium heat.
3. Drop spoonfuls of the mixture into the skillet and flatten slightly.
4. Fry until golden brown on both sides. Drain on paper towels before serving.

Methi Thepla (Fenugreek Flatbreads)

Ingredients:

- 1 cup whole wheat flour
- 1 cup fresh fenugreek leaves (chopped)
- 1/2 teaspoon turmeric powder
- 1/2 teaspoon red chili powder
- Salt to taste
- Water (as needed)
- Oil for cooking

Instructions:

1. In a bowl, combine flour, fenugreek leaves, turmeric, chili powder, and salt.
2. Gradually add water to form a dough.
3. Divide the dough into balls and roll each ball into a flatbread.
4. Heat oil in a skillet over medium heat and cook each flatbread until golden brown on both sides.

Savory Yogurt Pancakes

Ingredients:

- 1 cup yogurt
- 1/2 cup all-purpose flour
- 2 eggs
- 1 teaspoon baking soda
- Salt and pepper to taste
- Oil for frying

Instructions:

1. In a bowl, mix yogurt, flour, eggs, baking soda, salt, and pepper until smooth.
2. Heat oil in a skillet over medium heat.
3. Drop spoonfuls of the mixture into the skillet and flatten slightly.
4. Fry until golden brown on both sides. Drain on paper towels before serving.

Thai Scallion Pancakes

Ingredients:

- 2 cups all-purpose flour
- 1 cup boiling water
- 1/2 cup scallions (finely chopped)
- Salt to taste
- Oil for frying

Instructions:

1. In a bowl, combine flour and salt. Gradually add boiling water, mixing until a dough forms.
2. Knead the dough for a few minutes until smooth. Cover and let it rest for 30 minutes.
3. Divide the dough into equal parts, roll each part into a circle, and sprinkle with scallions. Roll tightly and flatten.
4. Heat oil in a skillet over medium heat, fry each pancake until golden brown on both sides.

Italian Polenta Pancakes

Ingredients:

- 1 cup cooked polenta
- 1/2 cup all-purpose flour
- 2 eggs
- 1/4 cup grated Parmesan cheese
- Salt and pepper to taste
- Oil for frying

Instructions:

1. In a bowl, mix cooked polenta, flour, eggs, Parmesan, salt, and pepper until well combined.
2. Heat oil in a skillet over medium heat.
3. Drop spoonfuls of the mixture into the skillet and flatten slightly.
4. Fry until golden brown on both sides. Drain on paper towels before serving.

Prawn and Chive Pancakes

Ingredients:

- 1 cup cooked prawns (chopped)
- 1/2 cup chives (chopped)
- 1/2 cup all-purpose flour
- 2 eggs
- Salt and pepper to taste
- Oil for frying

Instructions:

1. In a bowl, combine prawns, chives, flour, eggs, salt, and pepper.
2. Heat oil in a skillet over medium heat.
3. Drop spoonfuls of the mixture into the skillet and flatten slightly.
4. Fry until golden brown on both sides. Drain on paper towels before serving.

Savory Tomato Pancakes

Ingredients:

- 1 cup tomatoes (diced)
- 1/2 cup all-purpose flour
- 2 eggs
- 1/4 cup fresh basil (chopped)
- Salt and pepper to taste
- Oil for frying

Instructions:

1. In a bowl, mix tomatoes, flour, eggs, basil, salt, and pepper until combined.
2. Heat oil in a skillet over medium heat.
3. Drop spoonfuls of the mixture into the skillet and flatten slightly.
4. Fry until golden brown on both sides. Drain on paper towels before serving.

Couscous and Vegetable Pancakes

Ingredients:

- 1 cup cooked couscous
- 1 cup mixed vegetables (finely chopped)
- 1/2 cup all-purpose flour
- 2 eggs
- Salt and pepper to taste
- Oil for frying

Instructions:

1. In a bowl, combine couscous, vegetables, flour, eggs, salt, and pepper.
2. Heat oil in a skillet over medium heat.
3. Drop spoonfuls of the mixture into the skillet and flatten slightly.
4. Fry until golden brown on both sides. Drain on paper towels before serving.

Black Bean Pancakes

Ingredients:

- 1 cup black beans (cooked and mashed)
- 1/2 cup all-purpose flour
- 2 eggs
- 1/4 teaspoon cumin
- Salt and pepper to taste
- Oil for frying

Instructions:

1. In a bowl, mix mashed black beans, flour, eggs, cumin, salt, and pepper until well combined.
2. Heat oil in a skillet over medium heat.
3. Drop spoonfuls of the mixture into the skillet and flatten slightly.
4. Fry until golden brown on both sides. Drain on paper towels before serving.

Savory Crêpes with Ham and Cheese

Ingredients:

- 1 cup all-purpose flour
- 2 eggs
- 2 cups milk
- 1 cup ham (diced)
- 1 cup cheese (shredded)
- Salt and pepper to taste
- Butter for cooking

Instructions:

1. In a bowl, whisk flour, eggs, milk, salt, and pepper until smooth.
2. Heat a non-stick skillet with butter over medium heat, pour in batter to form a thin layer.
3. Cook until edges lift, then flip and cook the other side.
4. Fill with ham and cheese, fold, and serve.

Tandoori Chicken Pancakes

Ingredients:

- 1 cup cooked chicken (shredded)
- 1/2 cup all-purpose flour
- 2 eggs
- 1 tablespoon tandoori spice mix
- Salt to taste
- Oil for frying

Instructions:

1. In a bowl, mix shredded chicken, flour, eggs, tandoori spice, and salt until combined.
2. Heat oil in a skillet over medium heat.
3. Drop spoonfuls of the mixture into the skillet and flatten slightly.
4. Fry until golden brown on both sides. Drain on paper towels before serving.

Spinach and Ricotta Pancakes

Ingredients:

- 1 cup fresh spinach (chopped)
- 1/2 cup ricotta cheese
- 1/2 cup all-purpose flour
- 2 eggs
- Salt and pepper to taste
- Oil for frying

Instructions:

1. In a bowl, combine spinach, ricotta, flour, eggs, salt, and pepper until well mixed.
2. Heat oil in a skillet over medium heat.
3. Drop spoonfuls of the mixture into the skillet and flatten slightly.
4. Fry until golden brown on both sides. Drain on paper towels before serving.

Savory Pancakes with Roasted Red Peppers

Ingredients:

- 1 cup roasted red peppers (chopped)
- 1/2 cup all-purpose flour
- 2 eggs
- 1/4 cup feta cheese (crumbled)
- Salt and pepper to taste
- Oil for frying

Instructions:

1. In a bowl, mix roasted red peppers, flour, eggs, feta, salt, and pepper until well combined.
2. Heat oil in a skillet over medium heat.
3. Drop spoonfuls of the mixture into the skillet and flatten slightly.
4. Fry until golden brown on both sides. Drain on paper towels before serving.

Pesto and Parmesan Pancakes

Ingredients:

- 1/2 cup pesto
- 1/2 cup grated Parmesan cheese
- 1/2 cup all-purpose flour
- 2 eggs
- Salt and pepper to taste
- Oil for frying

Instructions:

1. In a bowl, combine pesto, Parmesan, flour, eggs, salt, and pepper until smooth.
2. Heat oil in a skillet over medium heat.
3. Drop spoonfuls of the mixture into the skillet and flatten slightly.
4. Fry until golden brown on both sides. Drain on paper towels before serving.

Savory Pancakes with Olive Tapenade

Ingredients:

- 1/2 cup olive tapenade
- 1/2 cup all-purpose flour
- 2 eggs
- 1/4 cup cream cheese (softened)
- Salt and pepper to taste
- Oil for frying

Instructions:

1. In a bowl, mix olive tapenade, flour, eggs, cream cheese, salt, and pepper until well combined.
2. Heat oil in a skillet over medium heat.
3. Drop spoonfuls of the mixture into the skillet and flatten slightly.
4. Fry until golden brown on both sides. Drain on paper towels before serving.

Radish Pancakes

Ingredients:

- 1 cup radishes (grated)
- 1/2 cup all-purpose flour
- 2 eggs
- Salt and pepper to taste
- Oil for frying

Instructions:

1. In a bowl, combine grated radishes, flour, eggs, salt, and pepper until mixed.
2. Heat oil in a skillet over medium heat.
3. Drop spoonfuls of the mixture into the skillet and flatten slightly.
4. Fry until golden brown on both sides. Drain on paper towels before serving.

Celeriac and Herb Pancakes

Ingredients:

- 1 cup celeriac (grated)
- 1/2 cup all-purpose flour
- 2 eggs
- 1/4 cup fresh herbs (chopped)
- Salt and pepper to taste
- Oil for frying

Instructions:

1. In a bowl, mix grated celeriac, flour, eggs, herbs, salt, and pepper until well combined.
2. Heat oil in a skillet over medium heat.
3. Drop spoonfuls of the mixture into the skillet and flatten slightly.
4. Fry until golden brown on both sides. Drain on paper towels before serving.

Sweet Corn and Zucchini Pancakes

Ingredients:

- 1 cup sweet corn (cooked)
- 1 cup zucchini (grated)
- 1/2 cup all-purpose flour
- 2 eggs
- Salt and pepper to taste
- Oil for frying

Instructions:

1. In a bowl, combine corn, zucchini, flour, eggs, salt, and pepper until mixed.
2. Heat oil in a skillet over medium heat.
3. Drop spoonfuls of the mixture into the skillet and flatten slightly.
4. Fry until golden brown on both sides. Drain on paper towels before serving.

Savory Pancakes with Greek Yogurt Sauce

Ingredients:

- 1 cup all-purpose flour
- 2 eggs
- 1 cup Greek yogurt
- 1/4 cup fresh dill (chopped)
- Salt and pepper to taste
- Oil for frying

Instructions:

1. In a bowl, mix flour, eggs, yogurt, dill, salt, and pepper until combined.
2. Heat oil in a skillet over medium heat.
3. Drop spoonfuls of the mixture into the skillet and flatten slightly.
4. Fry until golden brown on both sides. Drain on paper towels before serving.

Fennel and Orange Pancakes

Ingredients:

- 1 cup fennel bulb (finely chopped)
- 1/2 cup orange juice
- 1/2 cup all-purpose flour
- 2 eggs
- Salt and pepper to taste
- Oil for frying

Instructions:

1. In a bowl, mix chopped fennel, orange juice, flour, eggs, salt, and pepper until well combined.
2. Heat oil in a skillet over medium heat.
3. Drop spoonfuls of the mixture into the skillet and flatten slightly.
4. Fry until golden brown on both sides. Drain on paper towels before serving.

Chard and Cheese Pancakes

Ingredients:

- 1 cup Swiss chard (chopped)
- 1/2 cup cheese (grated, such as feta or cheddar)
- 1/2 cup all-purpose flour
- 2 eggs
- Salt and pepper to taste
- Oil for frying

Instructions:

1. In a bowl, combine chopped chard, cheese, flour, eggs, salt, and pepper until mixed.
2. Heat oil in a skillet over medium heat.
3. Drop spoonfuls of the mixture into the skillet and flatten slightly.
4. Fry until golden brown on both sides. Drain on paper towels before serving.

Coconut Curry Pancakes

Ingredients:

- 1 cup coconut milk
- 1/2 cup all-purpose flour
- 2 eggs
- 1 tablespoon curry powder
- Salt and pepper to taste
- Oil for frying

Instructions:

1. In a bowl, mix coconut milk, flour, eggs, curry powder, salt, and pepper until well combined.
2. Heat oil in a skillet over medium heat.
3. Drop spoonfuls of the mixture into the skillet and flatten slightly.
4. Fry until golden brown on both sides. Drain on paper towels before serving.

Bacon and Chive Pancakes

Ingredients:

- 1/2 cup cooked bacon (chopped)
- 1/4 cup chives (chopped)
- 1/2 cup all-purpose flour
- 2 eggs
- Salt and pepper to taste
- Oil for frying

Instructions:

1. In a bowl, mix chopped bacon, chives, flour, eggs, salt, and pepper until well combined.
2. Heat oil in a skillet over medium heat.
3. Drop spoonfuls of the mixture into the skillet and flatten slightly.
4. Fry until golden brown on both sides. Drain on paper towels before serving.

Savory Pancakes with Avocado and Salsa

Ingredients:

- 1 ripe avocado (mashed)
- 1/2 cup salsa
- 1/2 cup all-purpose flour
- 2 eggs
- Salt and pepper to taste
- Oil for frying

Instructions:

1. In a bowl, combine mashed avocado, salsa, flour, eggs, salt, and pepper until mixed.
2. Heat oil in a skillet over medium heat.
3. Drop spoonfuls of the mixture into the skillet and flatten slightly.
4. Fry until golden brown on both sides. Drain on paper towels before serving.

Mushroom and Spinach Pancakes

Ingredients:

- 1 cup mushrooms (sliced)
- 1 cup spinach (chopped)
- 1/2 cup all-purpose flour
- 2 eggs
- Salt and pepper to taste
- Oil for frying

Instructions:

1. In a bowl, mix sliced mushrooms, chopped spinach, flour, eggs, salt, and pepper until well combined.
2. Heat oil in a skillet over medium heat.
3. Drop spoonfuls of the mixture into the skillet and flatten slightly.
4. Fry until golden brown on both sides. Drain on paper towels before serving.

Savory Pancakes with Tomato Chutney

Ingredients:

- 1/2 cup tomato chutney
- 1/2 cup all-purpose flour
- 2 eggs
- Salt and pepper to taste
- Oil for frying

Instructions:

1. In a bowl, mix tomato chutney, flour, eggs, salt, and pepper until well combined.
2. Heat oil in a skillet over medium heat.
3. Drop spoonfuls of the mixture into the skillet and flatten slightly.
4. Fry until golden brown on both sides. Drain on paper towels before serving.

Green Onion and Bacon Pancakes

Ingredients:

- 1/2 cup cooked bacon (chopped)
- 1/4 cup green onions (chopped)
- 1/2 cup all-purpose flour
- 2 eggs
- Salt and pepper to taste
- Oil for frying

Instructions:

1. In a bowl, combine chopped bacon, green onions, flour, eggs, salt, and pepper until mixed.
2. Heat oil in a skillet over medium heat.
3. Drop spoonfuls of the mixture into the skillet and flatten slightly.
4. Fry until golden brown on both sides. Drain on paper towels before serving.

www.ingramcontent.com/pod-product-compliance
Lightning Source LLC
LaVergne TN
LVHW081502060526
838201LV00056BA/2897